ARCHAEOLOGY
The Study of Our Past

by Paul Devereux

Gareth Stevens Publishing
A WORLD ALMANAC EDUCATION GROUP COMPANY

CONTENTS

Please visit our web site at: **www.garethstevens.com**
or a free color catalog describing Gareth Stevens Publishing's
list of high-quality books and multimedia programs, call
1-800-542-2595 or fax your request to (414) 332-3567.

Library of Congress Cataloging-in-Publication Data

Devereux, Paul.
    Archaeology: the study of our past / by Paul Devereux.
        p. cm. — (Investigating science)
    Summary: Examines the science of archaeology and how it reveals the evolution
of human history by uncovering and studying the physical remains of the past.
    Includes bibliographical references and index.
    ISBN 0-8368-3228-0 (lib. bdg.)
    1. Archaeology—Juvenile literature. [1. Archaeology.] I. Title. II. Series.
CC171.D48   2002
930.1—dc21   2002022541

This edition first published in 2002 by
Gareth Stevens Publishing
 World Almanac Education Group Company
330 West Olive Street, Suite 100
Milwaukee, WI 53212 USA

This U.S. edition © 2002 by Gareth Stevens, Inc. First published by
ticktock Publishing Ltd., Century Place, Lamberts Road, Tunbridge Wells,
Kent TN2 3EH, U.K. Original edition © 2001 by ticktock Publishing Ltd.
Additional end matter © 2002 by Gareth Stevens, Inc.

Illustrations: John Alston, Simon Mendez
Gareth Stevens editor: Jim Mezzanotte
Cover design: Katherine A. Goedheer
Consultant: Robert J. Jeske, Associate Professor of Anthropology,
University of Wisconsin at Milwaukee

Printed in Hong Kong

2 3 4 5 6 7 8 9 06 05 04 03 02

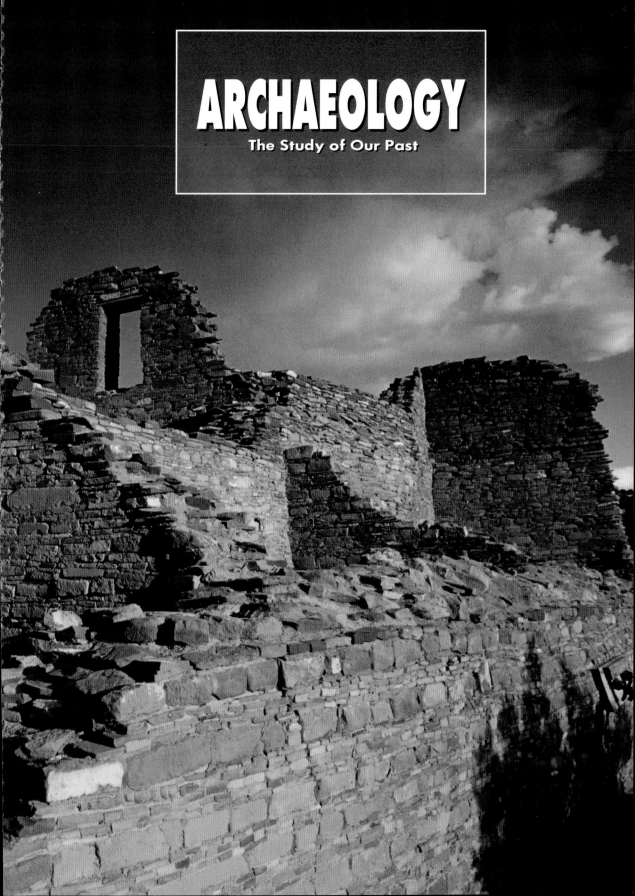

ARCHAEOLOGY
The Study of Our Past

WHAT IS ARCHAEOLOGY?

Archaeology is the study of the physical remains of the human past. Learning about the past helps us understand who we are and where we came from. Modern archaeology began in Britain at the end of the 17th century, when people began to study local ancient monuments, such as Stonehenge. In the 19th century, people began exploring suspected archaeological sites. At first, the digging was done crudely and without much care, but these early attempts gradually improved, and digging sites eventually became precise excavations. Since then, science has revolutionized archaeology.

THE CLUES

Archaeologists are detectives whose main clues are artifacts, features, and ecofacts. Artifacts are objects made or modified by humans, such as stone tools and jewelry. Each artifact can reveal a wide range of information, such as where it was made and what people ate at the time. Static features, such as places that were used for fires or to hold trash, can reveal a lot about how a community lived. Ecofacts are the remains of organisms.

PLANTS IN THE PAST

Plant remains are an important source of archaeological information. All flowering plants produce pollen (*right*), which consists of grains that are virtually indestructible. These tiny grains can reveal whether a particular area was hot, cold, dry, or wet. Plant remains can tell an archaeologist what crops were grown, what foods people ate, and even what herbal medicines were used at the time. The recovery, identification, and analysis of plant remains is called archaeobotany.

ANCIENT ADVENTURE

As scientists, most modern archaeologists are intellectual heroes, not colorful adventurers such as the fictional archaeologist "Indiana Jones" (*left*). Field archaeologists, however, occasionally encounter frightening situations. In the 1990s, for example, a group searching for a lost Mayan city in a Central American jungle was captured by revolutionaries. Fortunately, the archaeologists were eventually released unharmed.

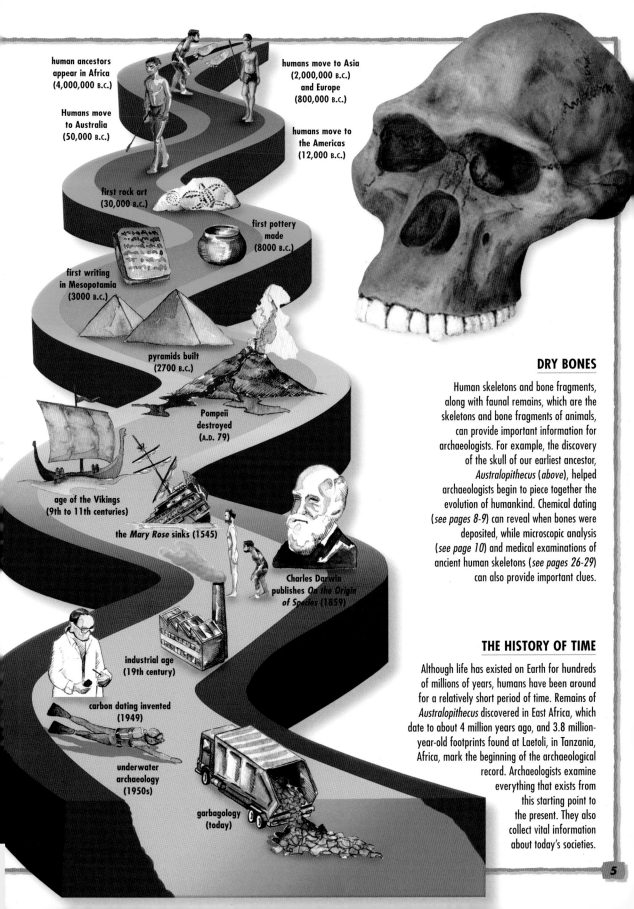

human ancestors appear in Africa (4,000,000 B.C.)

humans move to Asia (2,000,000 B.C.) and Europe (800,000 B.C.)

Humans move to Australia (50,000 B.C.)

humans move to the Americas (12,000 B.C.)

first rock art (30,000 B.C.)

first pottery made (8000 B.C.)

first writing in Mesopotamia (3000 B.C.)

pyramids built (2700 B.C.)

Pompeii destroyed (A.D. 79)

age of the Vikings (9th to 11th centuries)

the *Mary Rose* sinks (1545)

Charles Darwin publishes *On the Origin of Species* (1859)

industrial age (19th century)

carbon dating invented (1949)

underwater archaeology (1950s)

garbagology (today)

DRY BONES

Human skeletons and bone fragments, along with faunal remains, which are the skeletons and bone fragments of animals, can provide important information for archaeologists. For example, the discovery of the skull of our earliest ancestor, *Australopithecus* (*above*), helped archaeologists begin to piece together the evolution of humankind. Chemical dating (*see pages 8-9*) can reveal when bones were deposited, while microscopic analysis (*see page 10*) and medical examinations of ancient human skeletons (*see pages 26-29*) can also provide important clues.

THE HISTORY OF TIME

Although life has existed on Earth for hundreds of millions of years, humans have been around for a relatively short period of time. Remains of *Australopithecus* discovered in East Africa, which date to about 4 million years ago, and 3.8 million-year-old footprints found at Laetoli, in Tanzania, Africa, mark the beginning of the archaeological record. Archaeologists examine everything that exists from this starting point to the present. They also collect vital information about today's societies.

If archaeologists have an idea where buried artifacts might be found, they can use metal detectors. These tools can detect where metal artifacts or jewelry are buried.

An auger is a corkscrew-like tool with a T-shaped handle that can be rotated to bore into the ground. Augers can detect hollow areas underground that may be of interest to archaeologists.

Excavation destroys a site, so archaeologists keep careful records when on a dig. They record the exact position of each object. Soil that was swept up during a dig is put through a sieve to check for tiny bones or objects that might have been missed. Some soil is placed in water so seeds and other remains can float to the surface.

Once the archaeological layer of earth is exposed, workers carefully use trowels and fine brushes to scrape away the soil. Dental probes are often used to reveal delicate objects.

Ancient artifacts and bones are often extremely fragile, so they must be excavated with great care. Archaeologists carefully remove soil particles with a fine brush.

TRICKS & TECHNIQUES: INVESTIGATING A SITE

Archaeologists have gradually developed many techniques to help them find and survey sites. Some are very basic, while others require the use of scientific equipment. Once a site has been discovered, excavation can begin. A site plan is created, and the archaeologist then decides where to dig exploratory squares or trenches. They can be arranged on a grid layout so the exact locations of finds can be plotted. Excavated layers of earth are exposed in trench walls, like slices of cake.

To preview possible sites, archaeologists can study photographs taken from airplanes. Ground that has been disturbed usually holds moisture better than undisturbed land. This moisture affects vegetation, and dark crop markings are visible from the air. Buried building foundations or roads usually produce light crop markings.

Field walking involves systematically walking over plowed fields, searching the ground for fragments of pottery, flints, and other signs of human activity. Any finds are then plotted on a grid, so archaeologists can decide on the best places to start excavating.

Archaeologists use magnetometers and gradiometers to measure magnetic variations in the ground, which may indicate an archaeological site. They also use ground radar, which can produce a picture of an underground structure. Ground radar can detect a wide range of materials, such as metals, plastics, and ceramics.

magnetometer

gradiometer

ground radar

To find the best places to dig, archaeologists use resistivity meters, which measure moisture. The meters are attached to electrodes inserted into the ground. An electric current is then passed into the soil to provide a moisture reading. Buried building foundations, roads, and stone structures hold less moisture than solid ground, so archaeologists look for high resistivity, which indicates low moisture.

DATING TECHNIQUES

DENDROCHRONOLOGY

Dendrochronology is a technique that uses tree rings for dating. Since the rings of a tree each represent a year's growth, a tree's age can be determined by counting its rings. Tree-ring dating has produced some very precise dates. For example, by studying timbers found at a settlement site at Cortaillod-Est in Switzerland, archaeologists determined that the community was established with four houses in 1010 B.C. and expanded four times in subsequent years, and that a fence was added in 985 B.C.!

Archaeologists use several dating techniques. These techniques include dendrochronology, which involves examining tree trunks, and typology, in which an artifact's style is matched to a period of time. Chemical dating processes, which are more complex, can tell archaeologists how old something is by measuring carbon, minerals, or levels of radiation.

Plants take in carbon 14

Animals ingest carbon 14.

Humans ingest carbon 14 from plants and animals.

Remains of humans and other organisms become buried and are sometimes preserved.

Carbon 14 is in wood used for fires.

A QUESTION OF CARBON

All forms of life on Earth take in and store a radioactive substance called carbon 14. Since carbon 14 breaks down at a particular rate, the amount left in an organic sample can reveal how long ago an organism died. Archaeologists use a technique called radiocarbon dating to measure the amount of carbon 14 left in a sample, and thus find out its age. Geiger counters, or the more advanced accelerator mass spectrometry machines, measure carbon 14.

VOLCANIC CLUES

Potassium-argon dating works by measuring how quickly potassium has broken down. It is useful at sites near volcanoes, where our earliest ancestors laid down their footprints in cooling volcanic ash (*see pages 12-13*). Since the ash contains potassium, this technique can establish when the footprints were made.

STYLE SLEUTHS

The styles of artifacts have changed over time, and different cultures have different styles. Just as we can tell the difference in style between a car produced today and a car produced in the 1920s, archaeologists can determine the different time periods of pots, stone axes, and other artifacts. This technique is called typological sequencing.

ARTIFACTS & ARCHAEOLOGISTS

Artifacts are objects discovered in excavations and are often made of clay, stone, or metal. They are usually the most plentiful links to the past for archaeologists, because they tend to survive much longer than bone fragments or plant remains. Sometimes archaeologists can learn a lot from an artifact simply by examining it. When clues are not immediately obvious, however, archaeologists use more complicated techniques to unravel the past. These techniques range from chemical etching and microscopic analysis to DNA analysis and the use of computers and laser plotters.

UNDER THE MICROSCOPE

Archaeologists can use microscopes to find out more about a site. At Skara Brae, (*above*), a group of stone houses on the Scottish Orkney Islands dating from 3000 B.C., archaeologists found stone and shell cups with residues in them. Microscopic analysis revealed traces of milk and cereal products, providing clues about the diet of the people who once lived there. Traces of a red pigment were also found, suggesting rituals were held.

SECRETS OF LIFE

DNA is a chemical that contains the blueprint of life for all organisms. It is a set of special instructions for growth that makes all plants and animals distinct from one another. DNA is also a valuable resource for archaeologists. At Cuddle Springs in Australia, 30,000-year-old stone tools analyzed under an electron microscope revealed traces of blood and hair. DNA analysis showed that the traces were from a kangaroo, proving that the people of the time were able to hunt large animals.

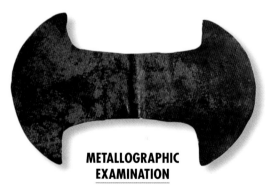

METALLOGRAPHIC EXAMINATION

Metallographic examination involves using chemicals to strip away a polished section of a metal artifact to reveal the metal structure beneath. Archaeologists then study the section under a microscope to learn what methods were used to make the artifact. This technique can also show if an iron tool or weapon was heated in charcoal to give it a hardened cutting edge. Metalworking in ancient times could be surprisingly sophisticated. The ceremonial bronze axe shown above is from the Mediterranean island of Crete. Chemical analysis has dated it to around 3000 B.C.

NEUTRON DETECTIVES

Neutron activation analysis can tell archaeologists exactly what something is made of and how and where it was made. Gamma rays are released by bombarding an artifact with neutrons. These rays are then measured to reveal crucial information. For example, archaeologists used this technique to examine ceramics (*right*) found at the Nazca site of Marcaya, in Peru, to find out if the ceramics had been made by the native population. The archaeologists learned that the ceramics were produced in a number of different ways and could not have been made at Marcaya.

COMPUTERS AND ARTIFACTS

In the picture shown above, an archaeologist is using a grid to study one of the Easter Island statues. The information that is gathered is then fed into a computer to produce a 3D image, which can be examined later. New technology is revolutionizing this aspect of archaeology. Portable laser plotters allow archaeologists to work quickly in the field and then take home incredibly accurate information.

RECONSTRUCTIONS

To learn more about artifacts, archaeologists sometimes try to recreate them in the way they would have been made in the past. Archaeologists have refitted flint blades to the stones they came from (*right*), in order to learn how the tools were made.

The complexity of the process shows that these tools were made by people who were quite sophisticated.

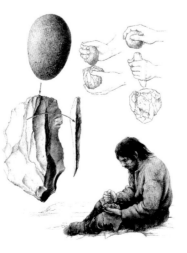

DATING POTTERY

Pottery pieces are some of the most plentiful artifacts available to archaeologists. Over time they steadily absorb radioactive elements. When these elements reach a very high heat, they begin to escape, in the form of a light energy known as thermoluminescence. To determine the age of a piece of pottery, archaeologists reheat a sample to measure the amount of light energy it contains and then convert the amount to a certain age. This process can date objects that are up to 80,000 years old.

DISCOVERING HUMAN EVOLUTION

Fossil bones and other evidence suggest that the ancestors of modern humans seem to have originated in Africa about four million years ago. Modern humans and their ancestors are classified as hominids. *Australopithecus* was the first hominid, succeeded by *Homo habilis*, then *Homo erectus*. Modern humans, known as *Homo sapiens*, appeared in Africa over 100,000 years ago and eventually spread out over the world. In Europe and Asia, *Homo sapiens* encountered another group of hominids, known as *Neanderthals*, who were slightly different. Around 30,000 years ago, the *Neanderthals* disappeared.

FOOTPRINTS FROM THE PAST

Our earliest ancestor was an ape-like hominid called Australopithecus. *In 1974, archaeologists in Ethiopia discovered the most complete* Australopithecus *skeleton ever found, dating back to at least 3 million years ago. They named the skeleton Lucy, after the Beatles song "Lucy in the Sky with Diamonds." In 1978, archaeologists discovered* Australopithecus *footprints in Tanzania that were 3.8 million years old. Two hominids, estimated to be shorter than 5 feet (1.5 meters) tall, had been walking together.*

THE *NEANDERTHAL* MYSTERY

Archaeologists have tried to figure out why the *Neanderthals* disappeared. *Neanderthals* may simply have been replaced by the smarter *Homo sapiens* or killed off by them. *Neanderthals* may also have merged with *Homo sapiens* through interbreeding. Archaeologists have discovered the skeleton of a young child with both *Neanderthal* and modern human traits.

NEW THEORIES

Between 1998 and 1999, archaeologists in Kenya discovered a fossil skull, jaws, and teeth that are as old as the skeleton of Lucy but are very different in appearance. From these remains, archaeologists have named a new species called Kenyanthropus. The size of the teeth and shape of the face indicate that Kenyanthropus had a different diet from Australopithecus, so these two species might have co-existed without competing with each other for food. Since scientists had previously thought that humans all evolved from a single common ancestor, this discovery shows that we still have a lot to learn about human evolution.

HOMO ERECTUS

Homo erectus first appeared 1.8 million years ago. Studies have indicated that the powerfully built *Homo erectus* may have been more efficient at walking than modern humans, whose skeletons have had to adapt to allow for the birth of larger-brained babies. *Homo erectus* skeletons have been found outside Africa, in Asia and Europe. Evidence suggests that *Homo erectus* probably used fire. The stone tools of *Homo erectus* are more sophisticated than those of *Homo habilis*.

HOMO HABILIS

Archaeologists have found a number of *Homo habilis* skulls, which have been dated to 2.4 million years ago. *Homo habilis* is often called "handy man," because of evidence of tools found with its remains. The average brain size of *Homo habilis* is much larger than that of *Australopithecus*, and from casts made of *Homo habilis* skulls, archaeologists have concluded that the brain shape is also more similar to modern humans. The area of the brain essential for speech is visible in one brain cast, indicating that *Homo habilis* was possibly capable of basic speech.

HOMO SAPIENS: MODERN HUMANS

Modern humans first appeared about 120,000 years ago. Casts made from the skulls of early Homo sapiens show that, compared to earlier hominids, they had a much larger brain capacity, which facilitates more complex thinking. About 40,000 years ago, tools became more sophisticated and were made with a wider variety of materials, such as bone and antler. Implements for engraving, sculpting, and making clothes also appeared.

STONE SIGNPOSTS?

Numerous boulders on wild moors in northern England and Scotland contain carvings that are thought to be from 3,000 to 4,500 years old. Archaeologists have noted that many of these boulders are located on prehistoric routes, which were used by hunters and, perhaps, those traveling to worship at moorland stone circles. The example shown above was discovered on the Scottish Isle of Westray.

SHIPS OF THE DEAD

Many ancient carvings exist on rock surfaces in Norway and Sweden, and they often feature images of ships (*right*). By comparing this art with other artifacts, archaeologists have determined that ships symbolized death. A ship used for burial on land was discovered at Oseberg in Norway, and a Viking cemetery at Lindhol Høje, in Denmark, contains almost 700 gravestones shaped like ships.

ETHNOARCHAEOLOGY

In some parts of the world, the beliefs and practices of traditional cultures can help archaeologists understand archaeological finds in nearby regions. In Australia, for example, where aboriginal art dates back to 20,000 years ago, archaeologists have learned quite a bit about this art simply by speaking to modern-day aboriginal artists who have carried on the ancient traditions. These artists have revealed that the hand stencils common in ancient aboriginal cave paintings are the mark of the artist or the sign of a visitor to the cave. Archaeologists also learned that many images in the caves relate to a belief system that modern aboriginals call "Dreamtime" — a time, they believe, when ancestral beings created the world. Ethnology and ethnography are studies of human cultures, and scientists who combine these studies with archaeology are known as ethnoarchaeologists.

THE FIRST WRITING

The Sumerians, who lived in a region called Mesopotamia in what is now Iraq, are believed to have invented writing about 5,000 years ago. Called cuneiform, this writing consisted of standardized marks on clay tablets (*right*). Archaeologists deciphered surviving examples of cuneiform in the 19th century. Many of the thousands of clay tablets turned out to be records of livestock, temple offerings, and items that were traded. Around the same time that cuneiform was being deciphered, French scholar Jean-François Champollion deciphered an ancient Egyptian writing, called hieroglyphics, through his study of the Rosetta Stone. Discovered in Egypt in 1799, the Rosetta Stone was covered with three kinds of writing — hieroglyphic, Greek, and demotic, which is another kind of ancient Egyptian writing. Because Champollion could understand the Greek and demotic writing, he was was able to figure out the meaning of the hieroglyphic text.

DECIPHERING ANCIENT ART & WRITINGS

Ancient art and writings provide exciting insights into the imaginations and thoughts of people in past civilizations. For generations, archaeologists have been studying these finds. Ancient art and writings often reveal a lot about the societies of their time.

EARLY ARTISTS

Cave paintings found in Lascaux, France (*above*), and Altamira, Spain date to about 30,000 years ago. At first, archaeologists believed the paintings were simply decorative, but many now think the paintings were a form of hunting magic — the artists painted animals they wanted to catch in order to bring good luck. After archaeologists discovered that the regions around the caves supported more people than they had previously thought, they introduced another theory — the caves may have been places of celebration where marriages and festivities were held.

KEEPING A RECORD

On excavation sites in northern Mesopotamia, archaeologists have found evidence of an early counting system (*above*) that existed about 8,000 years ago. The system consisted of a large clay ball with holes, called a bulla, and smaller tokens that could be inserted into the holes of the bulla. When the bulla was full, it was closed and sealed.

ARCHAEOLOGISTS & ANCIENT ASTRONOMY

The modern study of the ways ancient peoples used astronomy is known as archaeoastronomy. It began at the end of the 19th century, when British scientist Sir Norman Lockyer calculated that the axis of Stonehenge had been directed toward midsummer sunrise. In the 20th century, further research identified many ancient sites around the world that align with the Sun, the Moon, Venus, and stars such as Polaris, also known as the north or pole star, and Sirius, which is the brightest star. Experts believe that ancient peoples used astronomy mainly for ceremonial purposes rather than for scientific purposes.

MYSTERY CHAPEL

An ancient chapel cut out of rock (*above*) in Externsteine, Germany, has a small round window. Through this window, two mountain peaks mark the positions of the midsummer sunrise and the midsummer moonrise, at a point in the lunar cycle called the "major standstill" that occurs once every 18.6 years. The chapel was used either for Christian worship or as a pagan shrine.

WINTER SUN

The long passage of an ancient tomb (*above*) at Newgrange, Ireland, opens toward the rising midwinter sun. On the shortest day of the year, sunbeams penetrate the inner chamber, causing its stones to glow like gold. Perhaps this sunlight brought the promise of summer and rebirth during the dark depths of winter.

HEAVENLY WINDOWS

Casa Grande (*above*) is a mysterious building in southern Arizona that was used over 700 years ago by the Hohokam Indians. The structure may have been an observatory for maintaining a ceremonial calendar. Archaeologists have discovered that the square window on the right aligns with the southernmost setting position of the Moon, and that the round window on the left aligns with the midsummer sunset.

MIDSUMMER SUN

Construction of Stonehenge began almost 5,000 years ago. It was meant to tie in with the rise and fall of the Sun and the Moon. On a midsummer's morning, for example, the Sun would rise directly over the Heel Stone, located outside the circle. The first rays of light would shine into the center of the monument through the Horseshoe Stones (*right*).

THE AUBREY HOLES

Archaeoastronomers believe that the Aubrey Holes, which are holes arranged in a circle at Stonehenge, can be used to track the movement of the Moon. If a marker is moved around the circle by two holes every day, a cycle of the Moon is completed in the time it takes to complete the circle. It has also been argued that the holes can be used to predict eclipses. Moving a marker three holes a year completes a circle in the same time it takes for the Sun to come into alignment with the Moon — 18.6 years.

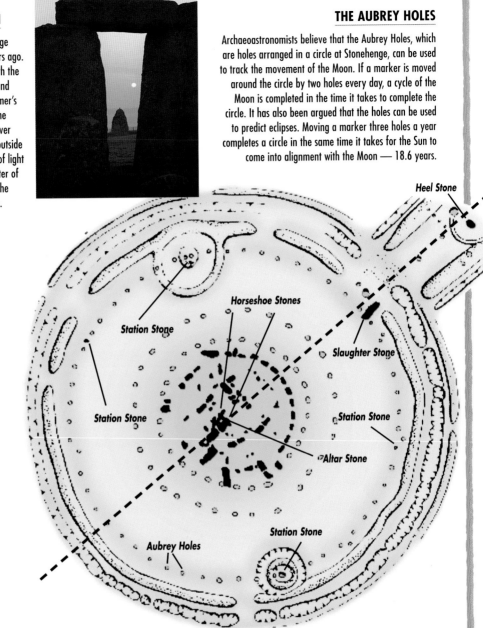

Heel Stone

Horseshoe Stones

Station Stone

Slaughter Stone

Station Stone

Station Stone

Altar Stone

Station Stone

Aubrey Holes

STONEHENGE ON THE MOVE

Stonehenge used to be aligned to a moonrise instead of the midsummer sunrise. The axis of the monument was physically moved around 2200 B.C. Calculations show that the orientation of an earlier entrance was toward the rising of the full midwinter moon, a key moonrise in the lunar cycle. The existence of this earlier orientation to a specific moonrise is further proof that the patterns found at Stonehenge are not random. The builders of Stonehenge intended for these patterns to tie in with what they observed in the sky.

VIKING DWELLINGS

The Icelandic sagas describe simple buildings made out of turf and stone. By comparing these descriptions with ruins found in Scandinavia and other parts of northern Europe, archaeologists have been able to create a detailed picture of what Viking houses probably looked like. They were single-story houses, with walls made from stone or staves (vertically-split tree trunks) and roofs made with thatch or turf. These dwellings would have been similar to buildings (*right*) located on the Scottish Shetland Islands.

IN FROM THE COLD

The Icelandic sagas were narratives created by Vikings who settled on Iceland (*above*), an island located in the northern Atlantic Ocean. The Vikings were explorers who were constantly in search of new lands. Viking explorations to Britain and northern Europe, as well as journeys to Greenland and beyond, are all described in the sagas. For centuries, archaeologists have been fascinated by the mention in the sagas of a settlement called "Vinland," which many believed was located in North America. The sagas speak of colonies founded by Thorfinn Karlsefni and Leif Ericsson. Using the Icelandic sagas as their primary guide, archaeologists tried to learn if the Vikings actually reached the Americas some five centuries before Christopher Columbus. Through the efforts of Norwegian historian Helge Ingstad in the 1960s, a settlement that was probably a Viking outpost was identified on the Newfoundland coast.

ANCIENT TEXTS: THE ICELANDIC SAGAS

Ancient texts can sometimes provide important clues for archaeologists. The Vikings came from Norway, Sweden, and Denmark. Also known as Norsemen, or "men from the north," they were at their most powerful between the 8th and 11th centuries. Archaeologists have found crucial information about their lifestyles, beliefs, and travels in ancient texts called the Icelandic sagas.

IN THE BOOK

The Icelandic sagas contain simple illustrations (*above*) that offer clues about what Viking warriors wore. These images, together with fragments of Viking clothing and helmets (*below*) that have been found, make it possible to draw a more accurate picture of how Vikings dressed. Clothing was probably simple and loose-fitting, while helmets were simple in design — they were not the elaborate, horned helmets that are popularly associated with Viking warriors.

DISCOVERING VINLAND

In the 1960s, Norwegian historian Helge Ingstad tried to find "Vinland," a settlement mentioned in the Icelandic sagas that was believed to be located in North America. Ingstad and his team explored the coast of Newfoundland, Canada. At a place called L'Anse aux Meadows (*above*), they uncovered the remains of eight turf-walled buildings. The largest house had walls 6 feet (2 m) thick, six rooms, and stone hearths. A piece of a tool for spinning cloth was discovered, offering evidence of Viking women, and radiocarbon dating indicated the settlement was from the early 11th century. It was probably a Viking outpost.

DECIPHERING LANGUAGE

Archaeologists have turned to language specialists for help in finding the "Vinland" mentioned in the Icelandic sagas. One expert suggested that "vin" means meadows, and that the North American Viking settlement was named after its rich meadows. Others suggested that "vin" referred to grapes, since grapes are mentioned in the sagas, but grape vines cannot be grown at L'Anse aux Meadows, and the earliest versions of the sagas do not mention grapes. Recently, however, Birgitta Wallace, who was in charge of the excavations at L'Anse aux Meadows, located a place south of the excavations where grapes could grow, in the Canadian province of New Brunswick. She suggests that the Vikings named the entire region they explored after this place.

UNDERWATER ARCHAEOLOGY

air balloon

Underwater archaeology involves the exploration of ancient wells and pools, sunken harbors, submerged cities, and ancient shipwrecks. Underwater finds are like time capsules for archaeologists because organic material, such as wood, usually survives longer beneath the water than on land. With recent advances in technology, archaeologists have made great progress in uncovering underwater sites, such as the *Mary Rose*, an English warship from the 16th century.

UNDERWATER EXCAVATION

Submersibles allow archaeologists to survey a site firsthand, while robot submarines allow them to explore from the safety of the ocean's surface. Once a site has been detected, divers wearing scuba gear can investigate. Before any excavation work begins, a 3D grid is placed around a site. Underwater blowers and suction pipes are used to clear away any debris and sediment. Underwater archaeologists then carefully map any finds using the grid. Special excavation techniques have also been developed to move artifacts. Underwater balloons filled with air, for example, can be used to lift heavy objects to the surface.

robot submarine

3D grid

SURVEYING AN UNDERWATER SITE

When surveying a submerged site, archaeologists tow various kinds of geophysical sensors behind a boat. Proton magnetometers can detect iron and steel objects, such as cannon balls and steel hulls, while special sonar can produce graphic images of features on the seabed. Archaeologists also use sound to search for artifacts. Sub-bottom profilers emit acoustic pulses that can detect objects beneath the surface of the seabed.

SAVING THE *MARY ROSE*

In 1982, the *Mary Rose* was raised from the ocean floor, where it had lain since 1545. After being towed into the Portsmouth naval base in England, it was wrapped in protective foam and polythene and constantly sprayed with water. The ship was housed in a dry dock that provided the right conditions for preservation. About half the starboard, or right-hand, side of the ship had been preserved, along with some of the decks. Archaeologists were able to learn about the diets of the sailors on the ship by studying sediments and bones recovered during the excavation. The sailors ate dried or salted cod, lamb, venison, and fresh fruit. Archaeologists also discovered carpentry tools and a medicine chest. Overall, the archaeological finds on the ship indicated that sailors of the period were relatively well-fed and well-treated.

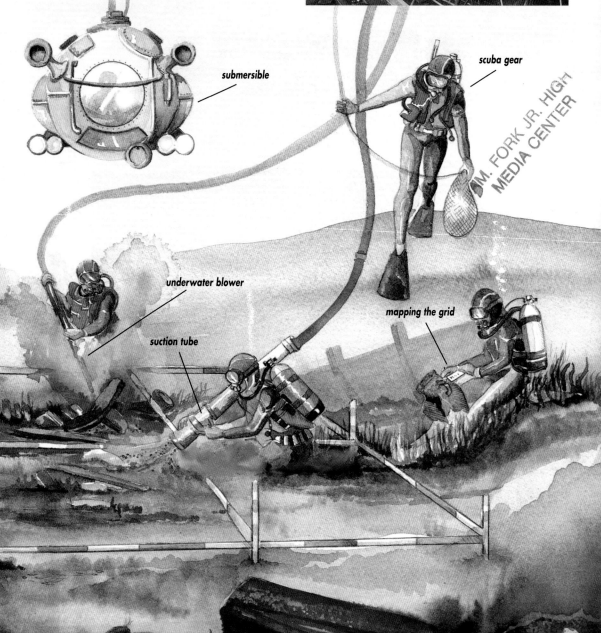

submersible

scuba gear

underwater blower

suction tube

mapping the grid

UNDER THE CANOPY

For years, archaeologists believed that the dense tropical rain forests of Costa Rica (*above*) hid archaeological remains. In 1985, to search for these remains, NASA conducted flights over the Arenal region of Costa Rica. Planes equipped with infrared cameras picked up some intriguing features. Using a thermal infrared scanner and photographs from a Landsat satellite, archaeologists determined that these features were footpaths (*right*) that dated from 500 B.C. — the oldest in the world. The paths were networks of human activity, and much evidence of that activity was later found along them.

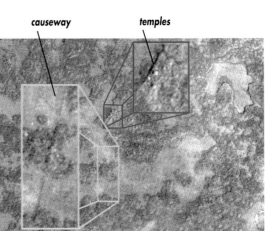

ancient footpath

causeway   temples

■ Forest   ■ Water   ▨ Forest Change 1990–1993
  Deforested   Wetland   Forest Change 1993–1995

THREATENED HERITAGE

Before the collapse of the Mayan empire in the ninth century, the Peten area of Guatemala was inhabited by millions of Mayan people. Within a few decades they had all vanished, but they left behind dramatic architecture. Today, the area is being threatened by human activity. Images from a Landsat satellite (*above, left*) reveal the extent of deforestation in the Peten. Archaeologists are making use of Landsat images to discover sites before they are destroyed. Because vegetation grows in a particular way around ancient ruins, and because ancient Mayan buildings are elevated features in a jungle area that is predominately flat, the Landsat images were able to highlight potential archaeological sites. Archaeologists spotted a causeway and temples (*above, right*) among the thick forest.

ARCHAEOLOGY FROM THE SKY

Archaeologists cannot always investigate a site thoroughly from the ground. Rain forests and other rugged environments, for example, often prevent archaeologists from exploring properly on foot, and sometimes discoveries are made only by chance. Today, however, remote sensing equipment such as Landsat satellites and thermal infrared scanners makes it possible to explore hard-to-reach areas from the sky. Pioneered by NASA, the U.S. space agency, this advanced equipment can peer through thick clouds, darkness, and even dense jungles.

prehistoric roads

CHACO CANYON

Between A.D. 900 and 1100, an ancient people called the Anasazi settled Chaco Canyon in New Mexico, and they left behind evidence of a highly sophisticated society (*below*). In 1982, NASA's archaeological research committee carried out a search for ancient roads using remote sensing technology. Although scientists and archaeologists alike were skeptical that the technology would be successful, the results were stunning. A thermal infrared scanner, which measures temperature differences near the ground, picked up over 200 miles (320 kilometers) of roads (*above*), ancient buildings, and agricultural fields.

GROUND TRUTHING

While remote sensing can provide archaeologists with invaluable clues as to where archaeological sites may lie, this technology does not eliminate the need for people on the ground to verify the information. This process of verification is called ground truthing. When ruins are revealed by remote sensing techniques, teams of archaeologists set out on foot to investigate.

MYSTERIES & FRAUDS

Sometimes the biggest challenge for archaeologists is searching out the truth. Many "ancient" artifacts are not quite what they seem, while other artifacts supposedly possess mystical, supernatural qualities. Through time-consuming research and the use of the latest scientific techniques, archaeologists have been able to separate the true puzzles of the past from those with more obvious explanations.

LEYLINES

In 1921, English businessman Alfred Watkins claimed that ancient sites were located on straight lines across the landscape called "leys." He thought they were prehistoric traders' tracks and claimed churches had evolved on certain marker points along the leys. In the 1960s, people rediscovered his theory, calling the lines "leylines." They fantasized that the lines were channels of some mysterious energy. Since Watkins's time, photographs taken from airplanes have discredited his theory. Most of the leys are chance alignments, while some result from medieval funeral paths leading to old churches. An ancient track in the Welsh mountains (*above, right*) leads to Llanthony Abbey.

ATLANTIS IN AMERICA?

Some people think that the presence of ancient pyramids in both Egypt and the Americas is proof that survivors from Atlantis, the fabled lost land in the Atlantic Ocean, must have spread east and west. The design of the pyramids in the Americas, however, is quite different from that of the Egyptian pyramids. Mayan pyramids in Mexico, such as the one at Chichen Itza (*right*), are also over 3,000 years younger than the pyramids in Egypt.

CROP CIRCLES

In the 1980s, strange geometric patterns began appearing in crop fields in England. Were these mysterious "crop circles" the landing marks of alien spacecraft? Humans could not possibly create these patterns...or could they? In 1992, an experiment showed that people could indeed make crop circles silently in the darkness of night. Special nighttime cameras were then used to catch people creating these circles. Some circle-makers are now quite open about their activities. One has even been arrested for causing crop damage!

NAZCA LINES AND ANCIENT ASTRONAUTS

Straight lines and other markings in desert areas around Nazca, Peru (*left*), have provoked much speculation. Some people claim these "Nazca lines" were runways for alien spaceships. While the desert markings are certainly remarkable, ancient spacemen are probably not the answer. The markings can easily be made by removing the darkened surface of the desert to reveal a lighter subsoil — the desert surface is so sensitive, even footprints can remain for centuries! Researchers now think the markings relate to religious practices of prehistoric Indians.

FAKE MUMMY

In October 2000, Pakistani national television announced that a 2,600-year-old mummy found in Kharan had been sold to the National Museum in Karachi. The mummy (*above*) was wrapped in an Egyptian style and rested in a wooden coffin decorated with cuneiform writing and images. When the cuneiform was fully translated, however, it turned out to be a copy of a previously discovered inscription, and a cuneiform expert determined that the inscription dated from no earlier than the 1930s. A full-body scan of the mummy revealed the corpse to be that of a 21-year-old woman who had been mummified for less than two years.

CASE STUDY:
ANCIENT EGYPTIAN LIFE

Even before archaeologists began investigating sites in Egypt in the early 20th century, people had long wondered about the magnificent landmarks built by the ancient Egyptians. Excavations yielded spectacular results — wonderful treasures and preserved bodies thousands of years old. Today, scientific advancements have enabled archaeologists to create a more complete picture of ancient Egypt, helping us to understand how the pyramids were built and what life was really like in this first great civilization.

THE SETTLEMENT OF EGYPT

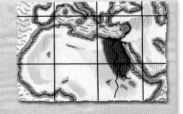

Since at least 5000 B.C., people farmed in the Nile Valley (*right, in red*), and tribal settlements gradually became more organized societies. Around 3050 B.C., the legendary King Menes unified all the settlements into one kingdom, which lasted for 3,000 years. Pyramids were at first built by trial and error, but by about 2500 B.C., when the famed Great Pyramid of Giza and its companions were built, the Egyptians had perfected their construction techniques.

ASRU THE MUMMY

When archaeologists examined a 3,000-year-old female mummy (*left*) found at Karnak temple in Egypt, they learned a lot about disease in ancient Egyptian times. Although the woman had probably lived a prosperous life, she had experienced many health problems. In particular, she had suffered from guinea worms, parasites that would have caused intestinal bleeding and diarrhea. The woman's legs had been amputated just before her death, probably as a result of trying to scratch out the worms. Her lungs contained a lot of sand, so she would have had great trouble breathing. X-rays indicate that she had arthritis in her hands and osteoarthritis in her back. No traces of painkillers were found in the body. Archaeologists do know, however, that the Egyptians used the blue lotus flower to help improve blood circulation, which would have helped ease the woman's pain.

LIFE FOR THE WORKERS

Archaeologists studying the pyramids at Giza (*above*) have recently learned some fascinating new information. By reading inscriptions found in the tombs, archaeologists now know that large, well-organized work crews were recruited to build the pyramids. Microscopic food residues indicate that workers were well fed on a diet of bread, fish, and beef, while decay in tooth specimens reveals that they also consumed a lot of beer and honey. Medical kits have also been found. This new evidence suggests that workers at the pyramids were treated better than was previously thought.

HOW MANY AND HOW LONG?

In A.D. 300, the Greek historian Herodotus stated that 100,000 workers were needed to build the Great Pyramid of Giza. To determine the accuracy of this number, archaeologists carried out an experiment using tools and techniques depicted on ancient Egyptian engravings (*above*). They determined that 40,000 workers probably could have built the pyramid in a timespan of ten years.

THE INTERNATIONAL MUMMY TISSUE BANK

In 1995, Rosalie David, the head of the Manchester Mummy Research Project, based in Britain, decided to set up an international mummy tissue bank. She requested mummy tissue samples from about 8,000 institutions around the world. The DNA samples collected will provide a unique insight into life in Ancient Egypt.

HARD WORK

DNA analysis of the bodies of workers found at the pyramids of Giza have revealed that they consisted of family groups. Cut marks on some of the bones indicate that many of the workers had broken arms, and some workers had limbs amputated. All of this evidence suggests that, however well the pyramid workers were treated, their lives were nonetheless very hard.

CASE STUDY: OTZI THE ICEMAN

In September 1991, the frozen remains of a 5,000-year-old man were found high in the Otzal Alps on the border of Italy and Austria. By studying the results of a medical examination, as well as artifacts found with the body, archaeologists were able to learn a lot about this man, nicknamed "Otzi." They recreated his last steps and discovered intriguing information about his diet, lifestyle, cause of death, and place of origin.

BIRCH FUNGUS

Archaeologists found pieces of birch fungus (*above*) in Otzi's backpack. The fungus contains antibiotic substances that can fight infection, so it was probably part of Otzi's "medical kit." Effective against various bacteria, including the bacteria that causes tuberculosis, the fungus was considered a powerful medicine in ancient Greece.

BONE DEGENERATION

Tattoo marks were found on Otzi's body, in areas such as his ankles and right knee, where he had been suffering from bone degeneration, or breakdown. The tattoos probably were part of a pain-relieving treatment. In folk medicine, it is widely believed that tattooing can help relieve pain in joints and muscles.

WEAPONRY

When Otzi died, he was carrying a bow and a dozen arrows in his quiver, or arrow container (*above*). Only two arrows were ready for use, however, and the quiver was damaged. The medical examination also suggests that Otzi had been shot by an arrow. He may have been recently involved in a skirmish. In his injured condition, perhaps he was forced to make a dangerous journey over the mountains. It was a journey he would never complete.

FINGERNAILS

The condition of Otzi's fingernails indicated that he performed manual labor. DNA analysis of the fingernails revealed that he probably suffered from crippling diseases, so perhaps he fell prey to the harsh weather of the Alps and froze to death.

LUNGS

A medical examination revealed that Otzi's internal organs were in good condition. His lungs were blackened, however, perhaps from regularly breathing smoke from fires.

DNA AND POLLEN SAMPLES

Almost as soon as Otzi was discovered, rumors began circulating that he was an elaborate hoax. Some even suggested that he was actually an Egyptian or South American mummy that had been planted in the Otztal Alps. DNA testing proved, however, that he did indeed come from Europe. Pollen samples extracted from Otzi's equipment helped pin down his origins still further. They indicate that he came from the Vinschgau Valley, which is located in northern Italy.

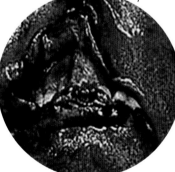

TEETH

Since Otzi's teeth were extremely worn down, archaeologists determined that he probably ate very coarse grain and used his teeth as a tool.

CLOTHING

Otzi's clothing confirms that he belonged to a sophisticated ancient culture. He had been well-dressed for his journey through harsh mountain conditions. Otzi had been wearing a fur cap, a sheepskin jacket, a weather-resistant, plaited-grass cape, leggings, and tough leather shoes that were insulated with grass.

CASE STUDY: POMPEII

In A.D. 79, the Roman city of Pompeii was buried under ash and lava when a nearby volcano, Mount Vesuvius, erupted. The eruption was a catastrophe for the city's inhabitants, but it was a gift to archaeologists of later generations. Pompeii was sealed and almost perfectly preserved by the lava, and it was left untouched until the 18th century. Early efforts at excavating the site were haphazard, and the ruins were raided for treasures. In 1860, however, Italian archaeologist Giuseppe Fiorelli supervised careful excavation and restoration work. Modern-day Pompeii, which is pictured at the bottom of this page and the opposite page, is built around the ancient city.

DAILY LIFE

The ruins of Pompeii offer many clues about what life must have been like for the inhabitants of the city at the time of the eruption. Mosaics and paintings on the walls of houses depict life in the city, and writings on the walls provide information on the price of goods, as well as the likes and dislikes of the people. Pompeii was a busy port town, full of shops, restaurants, and residential areas. The poor often lived in rooms above shops, while the rich lived in enormous houses with beautiful courtyard gardens.

PRESERVING THE EVIDENCE

In A.D. 79, lava and ash expelled by Mount Vesuvius buried the bodies of Pompeii's citizens. The ash then hardened around the bodies, forming molds. The bodies decayed, eventually leaving only hollow shells. Giuseppe Fiorelli came up with a way to recreate the bodies of these Pompeii victims from the shells. He made small holes in the hardened ash shells and poured in plaster of Paris. When the plaster hardened, Fiorelli chipped away the ash to reveal perfect casts of the bodies (left).

CULTURE

Pompeii had two amphitheaters, an example of which is pictured at left. One of the amphitheaters was large enough to hold up to 5,000 people. Mosaics show actors wearing masks and stage costumes, while writings on walls describe how much the people of Pompeii enjoyed the theater. Contests between professional fighters called gladiators were also a popular entertainment. A gladiator show at an amphitheater would include gladiatorial combat and fights between wild animals. Archaeologists have discovered helmets, shin protectors, and ankle guards, as well as writings on walls revealing that the citizens of Pompeii often treated gladiators as heroes.

BUYING AND SELLING

At the time of the eruption, Pompeii had many different types of shops. Artifacts and wall paintings reveal that potters, bronzesmiths, iron dealers, leather workers, butchers, and bakers all traded in the city. The city also had goldsmiths who sold luxury goods to the rich. Archaeologists have found many food shops, with stone counters (*right*) that probably held pots of food, water, or wine. Kettles, clay jugs, and bronze weighing scales have also been discovered.

FOOD AND DRINK

Although Mount Vesuvius was an ever-present threat, Pompeii's residents chose to plant crops on its fertile slopes. Wall paintings and writings indicate that they grew grapes, olives, and other crops and cultivated herbs, fruits, and vegetables in private gardens. They also raised sheep, chickens, and pigs. Pompeii exported wine to Rome, and archaeologists have discovered gold drinking vessels (*left*).

ARMCHAIR ARCHAEOLOGY

With the help of computer-aided design, or CAD, software, it is now possible to take a virtual tour of an archaeological site. Archaeologists feed digitized data obtained during an excavation into a computer. With that data, the computer is able to recreate the past. Hadrian's Baths were a Roman bathing complex constructed in A.D. 120. By using information obtained from the ruins of the site (*above*), archaeologists have created a virtual reconstruction of the original baths (*right*).

BRINGING THE PAST TO LIFE

"Living" museums allow visitors to interact directly with re-creations of life from the past. The Weald and Downland Open Air Museum (*left*) in England is a collection of 40 historical buildings, dating from the 14th century, that have been rescued from destruction. Each building was carefully dismantled at its original site and then rebuilt at the museum. Archaeologists recreated interiors in the style of the period, and they used written evidence and plant samples found at the original sites to plant gardens that are likewise faithful to the era. The museum includes a working water mill where stone-ground flour is produced daily, as well as a Tudor farm complete with livestock. Visitors can also watch demonstrations of traditional building and craft techniques.

ARCHAEOLOGY TODAY

Transformed by advances in science, the archaeology of today is more exciting than ever before. Archaeologists are now involved with everything from protecting and restoring important monuments to finding new ways to interest people in the past. They have helped create interactive, "living" museums, as well as computer-generated "virtual" tours on the Internet that allow people to visit archaeological sites from the comfort of their own homes. Today's archaeologists are also beginning to explore the recent past, examining industrial artifacts and even garbage to learn more about modern life.

1. Archaeologists made plans to move the temples of Abu Simbel from their original site.

2. A dam was built to protect the temples from the rising waters of Lake Nasser.

3. Piece by piece, archaeologists dismantled the temples and took them to a new location.

4. Finally, archaeologists put the pieces of Abu Simbel back together at the new location.

FINDING CLUES IN GARBAGE

Archaeologists of today explore the recent as well as the distant past. In the United States, for example, a branch of archaeology called garbagology has emerged. Garbagology involves the use of archaeological techniques to study the garbage of modern society, so that a more accurate picture of modern life can be created. At the University of Arizona, William Rathje and his team have studied thousands of tons of garbage in order to create a sophisticated database about U.S. society. The database contains fascinating information about the diets of the American people and the materials they use, as well as about differences that exist between the rich and the poor.

SALVAGE ARCHAEOLOGY

An important job for archaeologists today is protecting archaeological sites from damage caused by the environment or human activity. In Egypt, archaeological specialists from all over the world worked together to protect archaeological sites along the Nile that were threatened by a new dam being built in the area. After a comprehensive study, many temples were dismantled and rebuilt in safer places, while others were donated to museums.

GLOSSARY

archaeoastronomy: a branch of archaeology that involves the study of how ancient peoples used astronomy.

archaeobotany: a branch of archaeology that involves the study of ancient plant remains.

artifacts: objects made by humans.

Australopithecus: the earliest type of hominid.

cuneiform: the first known writing, which consisted of marks made on clay tablets.

dendrochronology: a dating technique that involves counting the rings of tree trunks.

ecofacts: the remains of living organisms.

ethnoarchaeology: the study of existing human cultures to better understand past cultures.

faunal remains: skeletons and bone fragments of animals.

features: stationary artifacts, such as buildings, that provide evidence of human activity.

garbagology: the study of garbage produced by modern societies.

gradiometer: an instrument that measures magnetic variations in the ground to pinpoint the locations of clay artifacts.

ground truthing: the verification of information from remote-sensing equipment by archaeologists on the ground.

hominids: a family of primates that includes *Homo sapiens* and their descendants.

Homo sapiens: modern human beings.

Landsat satellites: a series of satellites that have collected scientific data about Earth.

metallographic examination: the use of chemicals to strip away the surfaces of metal artifacts in order to learn how the artifacts were made.

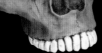

Neanderthals: early hominids who were slightly different from *Homo sapiens* and who disappeared about 30,000 years ago.

neutron activation analysis: a technique that can determine how and where a piece of pottery was made.

potassium-argon dating: a dating technique that measures the rate at which potassium in volcanic rock has broken down.

radiocarbon dating: a dating technique that determines how old the remains of organisms are by measuring how much carbon 14 they contain.

remote sensing: a technology that creates aerial images of possible archaeological sites with thermal infrared scanners, satellites, and other devices.

resistivity meter: a device that detects variations in underground moisture.

thermal infrared scanner: a device that creates aerial images by measuring temperature differences near the ground.

thermoluminescence: a form of energy that pottery gives off when heated, which can be measured to date pieces of pottery.

typological dating: a dating technique that involves comparing the styles of different artifacts.

uranium-series dating: a dating technique that measures calcium carbonate levels in rocks.

MORE BOOKS TO READ

Archaeology for Kids. Richard Panchyk
    (Chicago Review Press)

Archaeology Smart Junior. Karen Laubenstein
    (Princeton Review)

Eyewitness Books: Pyramid. James Putnam,
    James Punam (DK Publishing)

Finding the Lost Cities. Rebecca Stefoff
    (Oxford University Press)

Neanderthal Book & Skeleton. Stephen Cumbaa,
    et al. (Workman Publishing)

Stonehenge. Building History (series).
    Wendy Mass, Ed. (Lucent Books)

WEB SITES

Archaeology.
    www.ghcc.msfc.nasa.gov/archaeology/
    archaeology.html

Iceman: Mummy from the Stone Age.
    dsc.discovery.com/stories/history/iceman/
    otzi.html

Janet's Viking Site.
    www.schoolsite.edex.net.uk/587/ca/vikings/
    vikings.htm

Pictures of History: Pompeii.
    http://http.cs.Berkeley.EDU/~jhauser/pictures/
    history/Rome/Pompeii

INDEX

ACKNOWLEDGEMENTS

The original publisher would like to thank Advocate and Elizabeth Wiggans for their assistance.

Picture Credits: t=top, b=bottom, c=center, l=left, r=right
Ancient Art & Architecture Collection: 14/15c, 15t. Corbis Images: 9c, 11t, 10/11cb, 19t, 22t, 23b, 25cr, 26l, 27t, 27r, 30t, 30/31c, 31t, 31cr, 31c, 32t, 33b. Paul Devereux: 10b, 16t, 16b, 16/17b, 17t, 24t, 24b. Dr. Richard Hall: 19c. Kobal Collection: 4bl. Mary Rose Trust: 21t. Natural History Picture Agency: 18c. South American Pictures: 24/25c. Charles Tait: 4tl, 10t, 14t. South Tyroll Museum: 28/29. Weald and Downland Open Air Museum: 32b. Werner Forman Archive: 14c, 27c, 30b.

Every effort has been made to trace the copyright holders, and we apologize in advance for any unintentional errors or omissions.